50 Premium International Cheese Dishes for Home

By: Kelly Johnson

Table of Contents

- Fondue Savoyarde (Switzerland)
- Macaroni and Cheese (USA)
- Raclette (Switzerland)
- Croque Monsieur (France)
- Grilled Cheese Sandwich (USA)
- Lasagna (Italy)
- Poutine (Canada)
- Cheese Soufflé (France)
- Frittata al Formaggio (Italy)
- Queso Fundido (Mexico)
- Paneer Butter Masala (India)
- Cheese Grits (USA)
- Empanadas de Queso (Argentina)
- Mozzarella Sticks (USA)
- Caprese Salad (Italy)
- Brie en Croûte (France)
- Cheese and Herb Scones (UK)
- Cheese Croissant (France)
- Swiss Cheese Rösti (Switzerland)
- Cheese Fondue with Bread (Switzerland)
- Tarte Flambée (France)
- Gratin Dauphinois (France)
- Chiles Rellenos con Queso (Mexico)
- Spanakopita (Greece)
- Cannelloni with Ricotta and Spinach (Italy)
- Panzanella Salad with Feta (Italy)
- Cheese and Mushroom Quesadilla (Mexico)
- Mac 'n' Cheese Bites (USA)
- Salty Feta Cheese and Watermelon Salad (Greece)
- Cacio e Pepe (Italy)
- Baked Brie with Jam (France)
- Panzarotti (Italy)
- Halloumi Salad (Cyprus)
- Croquetas de Queso (Spain)
- Pizza Quattro Formaggi (Italy)

- Gratin of Cheese and Potatoes (Switzerland)
- Aged Manchego with Membrillo (Spain)
- Tzatziki with Feta (Greece)
- Cheese Empanadas (Chile)
- Blue Cheese Dressing (USA)
- Raclette with Charcuterie (Switzerland)
- Saganaki (Greece)
- Gougères (France)
- Moussaka with Cheese Bechamel (Greece)
- Cheese-stuffed Peppers (Turkey)
- Brie and Fig Tart (France)
- Panzerotti (Italy)
- Shepherd's Pie with Cheese (UK)
- Queso a la Plancha (Mexico)
- Pasticciotto (Italy)

Fondue Savoyarde (Swiss Cheese Fondue)

Ingredients:

- 1 1/2 cups Gruyère cheese, grated
- 1 1/2 cups Emmental cheese, grated
- 1 clove garlic, halved
- 1 1/2 cups dry white wine (e.g., Sauvignon Blanc or Swiss Chasselas)
- 1 tbsp lemon juice
- 1 tbsp cornstarch (optional, to thicken)
- 2 tbsp kirsch (cherry brandy) or water
- Freshly ground black pepper
- Freshly grated nutmeg
- Cubes of French baguette or other crusty bread for dipping

Instructions:

1. Rub the inside of a fondue pot with the garlic halves.
2. In a large saucepan, heat the wine and lemon juice over medium heat until hot but not boiling.
3. Gradually add the grated cheeses, stirring constantly until melted and smooth.
4. If the fondue is too thin, mix the cornstarch with the kirsch and stir into the cheese mixture to thicken.
5. Season with black pepper and nutmeg.
6. Transfer the fondue to the prepared fondue pot and keep warm over a low flame.
7. Serve with cubes of bread for dipping.

Macaroni and Cheese (USA)

Ingredients:

- 8 oz elbow macaroni
- 2 cups shredded sharp cheddar cheese
- 1 cup milk
- 1/2 cup heavy cream
- 2 tbsp butter
- 2 tbsp all-purpose flour
- 1/2 tsp mustard powder
- Salt and pepper to taste
- 1/2 cup breadcrumbs (optional, for topping)

Instructions:

1. Cook the macaroni according to package instructions, drain, and set aside.
2. In a saucepan, melt the butter over medium heat. Stir in the flour and mustard powder, cooking for about 1 minute to form a roux.
3. Gradually whisk in the milk and heavy cream. Continue to whisk until the sauce thickens, about 5-7 minutes.
4. Add the shredded cheddar cheese, stirring until melted and smooth. Season with salt and pepper.
5. Combine the cooked macaroni with the cheese sauce, stirring to coat.
6. If desired, top with breadcrumbs and bake in a preheated 350°F (175°C) oven for 15-20 minutes, until golden and bubbly.
7. Serve warm.

Raclette (Switzerland)

Ingredients:

- 1 1/2 lbs Raclette cheese, sliced
- 1 lb baby potatoes, boiled
- 1/2 lb pickled gherkins or cornichons
- 1/2 lb cured meats (e.g., prosciutto, salami)
- Freshly ground black pepper
- Fresh herbs for garnish (optional)

Instructions:

1. Set up a raclette grill or use a broiler to melt the cheese. Place the slices of cheese under the heat until it begins to melt and bubble.
2. While the cheese melts, boil the potatoes until tender.
3. Serve the melted cheese over the boiled potatoes and cured meats, along with pickles.
4. Garnish with freshly ground pepper and herbs if desired.
5. Enjoy the melted cheese with each bite of potatoes and accompaniments.

Croque Monsieur (France)

Ingredients:

- 8 slices of white bread
- 4 slices of ham
- 2 cups grated Gruyère cheese
- 1/2 cup béchamel sauce (recipe below)
- 1 tbsp butter
- Freshly ground black pepper

For the Béchamel Sauce:

- 1 tbsp butter
- 1 tbsp all-purpose flour
- 1 cup milk
- Pinch of salt
- Pinch of nutmeg

Instructions for Béchamel Sauce:

1. Melt butter in a saucepan over medium heat. Stir in the flour and cook for 1-2 minutes to form a roux.
2. Gradually whisk in the milk, stirring constantly until the sauce thickens. Season with salt and nutmeg.

Instructions for Croque Monsieur:

1. Preheat the oven to 375°F (190°C).
2. Spread a little butter on one side of each slice of bread. On the non-buttered side, layer ham and a slice of cheese.
3. Place two slices together to form sandwiches. Spread béchamel sauce on top and sprinkle with more Gruyère cheese.
4. Bake in the oven for 10-15 minutes, until golden and bubbling. Serve hot.

Grilled Cheese Sandwich (USA)

Ingredients:

- 2 slices of white bread
- 2 slices of American cheese (or cheddar, if preferred)
- 2 tbsp butter

Instructions:

1. Butter one side of each slice of bread.
2. Place a slice of cheese between the unbuttered sides of the bread.
3. Heat a skillet over medium heat. Place the sandwich in the skillet, buttered side down.
4. Grill the sandwich until golden brown on one side, about 2-3 minutes, then flip and grill the other side until golden and the cheese is melted.
5. Serve warm with a side of tomato soup for the classic pairing.

Lasagna (Italy)

Ingredients:

- 12 lasagna noodles, cooked
- 3 cups ricotta cheese
- 2 cups shredded mozzarella cheese
- 1/2 cup grated Parmesan cheese
- 2 cups meat sauce (prepared with ground beef, onion, garlic, tomatoes, and herbs)
- 1 egg
- Fresh basil for garnish (optional)

Instructions:

1. Preheat the oven to 375°F (190°C).
2. In a mixing bowl, combine ricotta, egg, and half the mozzarella cheese.
3. In a baking dish, spread a thin layer of meat sauce, then layer lasagna noodles, followed by the ricotta mixture, and a sprinkle of Parmesan and mozzarella.
4. Repeat layers until all ingredients are used, finishing with a layer of meat sauce and mozzarella cheese on top.
5. Cover with foil and bake for 25 minutes, then remove the foil and bake for an additional 10-15 minutes, until golden and bubbly.
6. Let cool for a few minutes before slicing. Garnish with fresh basil if desired.

Poutine (Canada)

Ingredients:

- 4 cups fresh French fries
- 2 cups cheese curds (preferably fresh white cheddar)
- 2 cups brown gravy (prepared with beef stock and thickened with flour or cornstarch)

Instructions:

1. Prepare the French fries according to your preferred method (deep-fried, baked, or air-fried).
2. While the fries cook, prepare the brown gravy by simmering beef stock and thickening it with flour or cornstarch.
3. Place the hot fries on a plate or dish. Sprinkle the cheese curds over the fries.
4. Pour the hot gravy over the fries and cheese curds.
5. Serve immediately while the cheese curds are melting.

Cheese Soufflé (France)

Ingredients:

- 2 tbsp butter
- 2 tbsp flour
- 1 cup milk
- 1 1/2 cups grated Gruyère cheese
- 4 large eggs, separated
- 1/4 tsp mustard powder
- Salt and pepper to taste
- A pinch of cayenne pepper (optional)

Instructions:

1. Preheat the oven to 375°F (190°C). Grease a soufflé dish with butter and dust with flour.
2. In a saucepan, melt butter over medium heat. Stir in the flour and cook for 1-2 minutes to form a roux.
3. Gradually add the milk, whisking constantly until thickened. Remove from heat and stir in the cheese, egg yolks, mustard, cayenne, salt, and pepper.
4. In a separate bowl, beat the egg whites until stiff peaks form. Gently fold the egg whites into the cheese mixture.
5. Pour the mixture into the prepared soufflé dish and bake for 20-25 minutes, or until puffed and golden brown.
6. Serve immediately.

Frittata al Formaggio (Italy)

Ingredients:

- 6 large eggs
- 1 cup grated Parmesan cheese
- 1/2 cup shredded mozzarella cheese
- 1/2 cup heavy cream
- 1/2 cup sautéed vegetables (e.g., spinach, mushrooms, bell peppers)
- 1 tbsp olive oil
- Salt and pepper to taste

Instructions:

1. Preheat the oven to 375°F (190°C).
2. In a mixing bowl, whisk together the eggs, Parmesan, mozzarella, heavy cream, salt, and pepper.
3. Heat olive oil in an ovenproof skillet over medium heat. Add the sautéed vegetables and cook for 1-2 minutes to warm through.
4. Pour the egg mixture over the vegetables in the skillet. Stir gently to combine.
5. Transfer the skillet to the oven and bake for 12-15 minutes, or until the frittata is set and lightly golden.
6. Let cool slightly, then slice and serve warm.

Queso Fundido (Mexico)

Ingredients:

- 2 cups shredded Oaxaca cheese (or a combination of Monterey Jack and mozzarella)
- 1/2 cup chorizo, cooked and crumbled
- 1/2 onion, finely chopped
- 1 small bell pepper, chopped
- Fresh cilantro for garnish
- Tortilla chips or warm tortillas for serving

Instructions:

1. In a skillet, cook the chorizo over medium heat until browned. Remove from the pan and set aside.
2. In the same skillet, sauté the onion and bell pepper until softened.
3. Add the shredded cheese to the skillet and cook, stirring occasionally, until the cheese is melted and bubbling.
4. Return the cooked chorizo to the skillet and stir to combine.
5. Garnish with fresh cilantro and serve with tortilla chips or warm tortillas for dipping.

Paneer Butter Masala (India)

Ingredients:

- 1 lb paneer, cubed
- 2 tbsp butter
- 1 onion, finely chopped
- 1 cup tomato puree
- 1/2 cup heavy cream
- 1 tsp garam masala
- 1 tsp ground cumin
- 1 tsp chili powder
- Salt to taste
- Fresh cilantro for garnish

Instructions:

1. Heat the butter in a large pan over medium heat. Add the chopped onion and cook until softened and golden.
2. Stir in the tomato puree, garam masala, cumin, chili powder, and salt. Cook for 5 minutes, stirring occasionally.
3. Add the paneer cubes and cook for an additional 5-7 minutes.
4. Stir in the heavy cream and cook for another 5 minutes until the sauce is thick and creamy.
5. Garnish with fresh cilantro and serve with naan or rice.

Cheese Grits (USA)

Ingredients:

- 1 cup grits (stone-ground or quick-cooking)
- 4 cups water
- 2 tbsp butter
- 2 cups shredded sharp cheddar cheese
- 1/2 cup milk or cream
- Salt and pepper to taste

Instructions:

1. Bring the water to a boil in a large pot. Slowly whisk in the grits, reduce heat to low, and cook, stirring occasionally, for 5-10 minutes (depending on the type of grits).
2. Once the grits are cooked and tender, stir in the butter, cheese, and milk. Continue to cook until the cheese has melted and the mixture is creamy.
3. Season with salt and pepper to taste, and serve warm as a side dish.

Empanadas de Queso (Argentina)

Ingredients:

- 1 package of empanada dough discs
- 2 cups crumbled feta cheese (or a mix of mozzarella and cheddar)
- 1/4 cup finely chopped fresh parsley
- 1 egg, beaten (for egg wash)
- Olive oil for frying

Instructions:

1. In a bowl, mix the crumbled cheese and chopped parsley.
2. Place a spoonful of the cheese mixture in the center of each empanada dough disc.
3. Fold the dough over to form a half-moon shape and press the edges to seal tightly.
4. Heat olive oil in a frying pan over medium heat. Fry the empanadas in batches until golden brown on both sides, about 3-4 minutes per side.
5. Drain on paper towels and serve warm.

Mozzarella Sticks (USA)

Ingredients:

- 12 oz mozzarella cheese sticks, cut in half
- 1 cup all-purpose flour
- 2 large eggs, beaten
- 1 cup breadcrumbs (preferably panko)
- 1/2 tsp garlic powder
- 1/2 tsp onion powder
- Salt and pepper to taste
- Vegetable oil for frying
- Marinara sauce for dipping

Instructions:

1. Dredge each mozzarella stick in flour, then dip in the beaten eggs, and coat with breadcrumbs.
2. Freeze the breaded mozzarella sticks for at least 30 minutes to prevent them from melting too quickly during frying.
3. Heat oil in a deep frying pan over medium-high heat. Fry the mozzarella sticks in batches until golden and crispy, about 2-3 minutes per batch.
4. Drain on paper towels and serve with marinara sauce for dipping.

Caprese Salad (Italy)

Ingredients:

- 3 large ripe tomatoes, sliced
- 8 oz fresh mozzarella cheese, sliced
- Fresh basil leaves
- Extra virgin olive oil
- Balsamic vinegar (optional)
- Salt and freshly ground black pepper

Instructions:

1. On a large plate, arrange alternating slices of tomato, mozzarella, and fresh basil.
2. Drizzle with olive oil and balsamic vinegar (if using).
3. Season with salt and pepper to taste.
4. Serve immediately as a fresh appetizer or side dish.

Brie en Croûte (France)

Ingredients:

- 1 wheel of Brie cheese (8 oz)
- 1 sheet of puff pastry
- 2 tbsp fruit preserves (e.g., apricot or raspberry)
- 1 egg (for egg wash)

Instructions:

1. Preheat the oven to 375°F (190°C).
2. Unroll the puff pastry on a parchment-lined baking sheet.
3. Place the Brie cheese in the center of the pastry and spread fruit preserves on top of the cheese.
4. Fold the pastry over the Brie to enclose it, sealing the edges.
5. Brush the pastry with beaten egg for a golden finish.
6. Bake for 25-30 minutes, or until the puff pastry is golden brown.
7. Let cool for 5 minutes before serving with crackers or sliced baguette.

Cheese and Herb Scones (UK)

Ingredients:

- 2 cups all-purpose flour
- 1 tbsp baking powder
- 1/2 tsp salt
- 1/4 tsp freshly ground black pepper
- 1/2 cup cold unsalted butter, cubed
- 1 cup grated sharp cheddar cheese
- 2 tbsp fresh chives, chopped
- 1/2 cup milk
- 1 egg (for egg wash)

Instructions:

1. Preheat the oven to 400°F (200°C).
2. In a large bowl, combine the flour, baking powder, salt, and pepper. Add the cold butter and rub it into the flour until the mixture resembles coarse crumbs.
3. Stir in the grated cheese and chopped chives.
4. Make a well in the center and pour in the milk. Stir gently to form a dough.
5. Turn the dough out onto a lightly floured surface and gently roll or pat it to about 1-inch thickness. Cut into rounds with a biscuit cutter.
6. Place the scones on a baking sheet and brush with beaten egg.
7. Bake for 15-20 minutes, or until golden brown. Serve warm.

Cheese Croissant (France)

Ingredients:

- 1 sheet of puff pastry (or pre-made croissant dough)
- 1 cup grated Gruyère cheese
- 1/4 cup cream cheese (optional, for extra creaminess)
- 1 egg (for egg wash)
- Salt and pepper to taste

Instructions:

1. Preheat the oven to 375°F (190°C).
2. Roll out the puff pastry or croissant dough on a lightly floured surface. Cut it into triangles (or use pre-shaped croissant dough).
3. Place a small amount of grated Gruyère and a teaspoon of cream cheese in the center of each triangle.
4. Roll the dough up from the wider edge to form croissants.
5. Brush the croissants with a beaten egg for a golden finish.
6. Bake for 15-20 minutes, or until golden and puffed.
7. Serve warm with a touch of salt and pepper.

Swiss Cheese Rösti (Switzerland)

Ingredients:

- 4 large russet potatoes, peeled and grated
- 1/2 cup grated Gruyère cheese
- 2 tbsp butter
- 1 small onion, finely chopped
- Salt and pepper to taste

Instructions:

1. Place the grated potatoes in a clean towel and squeeze out excess moisture.
2. In a large skillet, melt butter over medium heat. Add the onions and sauté until soft.
3. Add the grated potatoes to the skillet and cook for about 10-12 minutes, stirring occasionally, until crispy and golden.
4. Stir in the Gruyère cheese, salt, and pepper, and cook for an additional 2-3 minutes.
5. Flip the rösti over and cook for another 5-6 minutes until golden on both sides.
6. Serve warm, garnished with fresh herbs if desired.

Cheese Fondue with Bread (Switzerland)

Ingredients:

- 1 lb Gruyère cheese, grated
- 1/2 lb Emmental cheese, grated
- 1 cup dry white wine
- 1 garlic clove, halved
- 1 tbsp lemon juice
- 1 tbsp cornstarch
- 1/4 cup kirsch (cherry brandy, optional)
- Freshly ground black pepper and nutmeg to taste
- 1 loaf crusty French bread, cut into cubes

Instructions:

1. Rub the inside of a fondue pot with the cut sides of the garlic.
2. In a small bowl, mix the grated cheeses with the cornstarch. Set aside.
3. Heat the wine and lemon juice in the fondue pot over medium heat until warm.
4. Gradually add the cheese mixture to the wine, stirring constantly until smooth and melted.
5. If desired, stir in the kirsch for added flavor and smoothness.
6. Season with pepper and nutmeg to taste.
7. Serve the fondue with cubes of bread for dipping.

Tarte Flambée (France)

Ingredients:

- 1 pizza dough or thin tart crust
- 1/2 cup crème fraîche or sour cream
- 1/2 large onion, thinly sliced
- 4 oz lardons or bacon, diced
- 1 cup grated Gruyère cheese
- Salt and pepper to taste

Instructions:

1. Preheat the oven to 475°F (245°C).
2. Roll out the pizza dough or tart crust onto a baking sheet lined with parchment paper.
3. Spread a thin layer of crème fraîche or sour cream over the dough.
4. Evenly distribute the sliced onions and lardons over the crème fraîche.
5. Sprinkle the grated Gruyère cheese over the top, and season with salt and pepper.
6. Bake for 10-12 minutes until the crust is golden and the cheese is bubbling.
7. Serve immediately as a savory appetizer or main dish.

Gratin Dauphinois (France)

Ingredients:

- 4 large Yukon Gold potatoes, thinly sliced
- 2 cups heavy cream
- 1 cup whole milk
- 1 garlic clove, minced
- 1 1/2 cups grated Gruyère cheese
- 1/2 tsp nutmeg
- Salt and pepper to taste
- 1 tbsp butter (for greasing)

Instructions:

1. Preheat the oven to 375°F (190°C). Grease a baking dish with butter.
2. In a saucepan, heat the cream, milk, garlic, nutmeg, salt, and pepper over medium heat until warm.
3. Layer the thinly sliced potatoes in the prepared baking dish, slightly overlapping each layer.
4. Pour the warm cream mixture over the potatoes, ensuring they are fully covered.
5. Sprinkle the grated Gruyère cheese on top of the potatoes.
6. Bake for 45-50 minutes, or until the top is golden and bubbly, and the potatoes are tender.
7. Let rest for a few minutes before serving.

Chiles Rellenos con Queso (Mexico)

Ingredients:

- 6 poblano peppers
- 1 cup Oaxaca cheese (or mozzarella)
- 2 eggs, separated
- 1/4 cup flour
- 1/2 cup vegetable oil for frying
- Salt to taste
- Tomato sauce (optional, for serving)

Instructions:

1. Roast the poblano peppers over an open flame until the skin is blackened. Place them in a sealed plastic bag to steam for 10 minutes, then peel off the skins and remove the seeds.
2. Stuff each pepper with Oaxaca cheese, then set aside.
3. In a bowl, whisk the egg whites until stiff peaks form. In another bowl, whisk the yolks with a pinch of salt.
4. Gently fold the egg yolks into the whipped egg whites.
5. Dredge the stuffed peppers in flour, then dip them in the egg mixture.
6. Heat oil in a frying pan over medium heat and fry the peppers until golden and crispy, about 3-4 minutes per side.
7. Drain on paper towels and serve with tomato sauce if desired.

Spanakopita (Greece)

Ingredients:

- 1 lb fresh spinach, chopped
- 1/2 cup feta cheese, crumbled
- 1/2 cup ricotta cheese
- 1/4 cup fresh dill, chopped
- 1/4 cup onions, finely chopped
- 1/2 lb phyllo dough (about 8 sheets)
- 1/4 cup olive oil
- Salt and pepper to taste

Instructions:

1. Preheat the oven to 375°F (190°C).
2. In a pan, sauté the onions and spinach until the spinach is wilted and the onions are soft.
3. Remove from heat and stir in the feta, ricotta, dill, salt, and pepper.
4. Brush a baking dish with olive oil and layer a sheet of phyllo dough, brushing each sheet with more olive oil. Layer 4 sheets in total.
5. Spread the spinach and cheese mixture over the dough.
6. Cover with the remaining phyllo sheets, brushing each with olive oil.
7. Bake for 30-35 minutes, or until golden and crisp. Let cool before cutting into squares.

Cannelloni with Ricotta and Spinach (Italy)

Ingredients:

- 12 cannelloni pasta tubes
- 2 cups ricotta cheese
- 1 lb fresh spinach, sautéed and chopped
- 1 egg
- 1/2 cup grated Parmesan cheese
- 2 cups marinara sauce
- 1 cup shredded mozzarella cheese

Instructions:

1. Preheat the oven to 375°F (190°C).
2. Cook the cannelloni pasta according to package directions, then drain and cool slightly.
3. In a bowl, mix the ricotta, spinach, egg, Parmesan, salt, and pepper.
4. Stuff each cannelloni tube with the ricotta mixture.
5. Spread half of the marinara sauce in the bottom of a baking dish. Arrange the stuffed cannelloni on top.
6. Pour the remaining marinara sauce over the top and sprinkle with mozzarella cheese.
7. Cover with foil and bake for 25 minutes. Remove the foil and bake for an additional 10 minutes until bubbly and golden.
8. Serve hot.

Panzanella Salad with Feta (Italy)

Ingredients:

- 4 cups cubed day-old Italian bread
- 2 cups cherry tomatoes, halved
- 1 cucumber, chopped
- 1/4 red onion, thinly sliced
- 1/2 cup feta cheese, crumbled
- 2 tbsp olive oil
- 1 tbsp red wine vinegar
- Salt and pepper to taste
- Fresh basil leaves for garnish

Instructions:

1. In a large bowl, toss the cubed bread with olive oil and bake at 375°F (190°C) for 10-12 minutes, until golden and crispy.
2. In a separate bowl, combine the tomatoes, cucumber, onion, and feta.
3. Once the bread is toasted, add it to the vegetable mixture and toss gently.
4. Drizzle with olive oil, red wine vinegar, salt, and pepper.
5. Garnish with fresh basil leaves and serve immediately.

Cheese and Mushroom Quesadilla (Mexico)

Ingredients:

- 4 large flour tortillas
- 1 cup shredded cheddar cheese
- 1 cup shredded mozzarella cheese
- 1 cup sliced mushrooms (button or cremini)
- 1 small onion, thinly sliced
- 1 tbsp olive oil
- 1/4 tsp cumin (optional)
- Salt and pepper to taste
- Sour cream and salsa for serving

Instructions:

1. Heat olive oil in a pan over medium heat. Add the sliced mushrooms and onions, sautéing until softened and golden, about 5-7 minutes.
2. Season with cumin, salt, and pepper. Remove from heat.
3. Place a tortilla in a hot skillet. Add a layer of cheese, followed by the mushroom-onion mixture. Top with another layer of cheese and cover with another tortilla.
4. Cook on each side for 2-3 minutes until the tortillas are golden and the cheese has melted.
5. Serve warm with sour cream and salsa.

Mac 'n' Cheese Bites (USA)

Ingredients:

- 2 cups cooked elbow macaroni
- 2 cups shredded cheddar cheese
- 1/2 cup milk
- 2 eggs, beaten
- 1/2 cup breadcrumbs
- 1/2 cup grated Parmesan cheese
- 1 tbsp butter
- Salt and pepper to taste
- Vegetable oil for frying

Instructions:

1. In a saucepan, melt butter over medium heat and stir in the milk and cheddar cheese until melted and smooth.
2. Mix the cooked macaroni into the cheesy sauce. Remove from heat and let cool slightly.
3. Stir in the eggs, breadcrumbs, Parmesan cheese, salt, and pepper. Form the mixture into small bite-sized balls.
4. Heat vegetable oil in a deep fryer or large pan to 375°F (190°C).
5. Fry the mac 'n' cheese bites for 2-3 minutes, or until golden and crispy.
6. Drain on paper towels and serve warm with dipping sauces.

Salty Feta Cheese and Watermelon Salad (Greece)

Ingredients:

- 2 cups watermelon, cut into cubes
- 1 cup feta cheese, crumbled
- 1/2 small red onion, thinly sliced
- 1/4 cup fresh mint leaves, chopped
- 2 tbsp olive oil
- 1 tbsp red wine vinegar
- Salt and black pepper to taste

Instructions:

1. In a large bowl, combine the watermelon cubes, crumbled feta, red onion, and mint leaves.
2. Drizzle with olive oil and red wine vinegar, and gently toss to combine.
3. Season with salt and black pepper to taste.
4. Serve immediately or refrigerate for 30 minutes before serving.

Cacio e Pepe (Italy)

Ingredients:

- 1 lb spaghetti
- 1 cup Pecorino Romano cheese, finely grated
- 1 tsp black pepper, freshly cracked
- Salt to taste
- 1/4 cup pasta cooking water

Instructions:

1. Cook the spaghetti in salted boiling water until al dente. Reserve 1/4 cup of pasta cooking water and drain the rest.
2. Return the pasta to the pot over low heat. Add the reserved pasta water and black pepper.
3. Gradually stir in the Pecorino Romano cheese until the pasta is well coated and creamy.
4. Adjust seasoning with salt and pepper.
5. Serve immediately, garnished with more grated cheese if desired.

Baked Brie with Jam (France)

Ingredients:

- 1 wheel of Brie cheese (about 8 oz)
- 2 tbsp fruit jam (apricot, raspberry, or fig)
- 1/4 cup chopped nuts (pecans, almonds, or walnuts)
- 1 tbsp honey
- Crackers or baguette slices for serving

Instructions:

1. Preheat the oven to 350°F (175°C).
2. Place the Brie cheese on a baking sheet lined with parchment paper.
3. Spread the fruit jam on top of the Brie and sprinkle with chopped nuts.
4. Drizzle with honey and bake for 10-15 minutes, or until the cheese is melted and the top is golden.
5. Serve warm with crackers or baguette slices.

Panzarotti (Italy)

Ingredients:

- 1 lb pizza dough
- 1 cup mozzarella cheese, shredded
- 1/2 cup ricotta cheese
- 1/4 cup Parmesan cheese, grated
- 1/4 cup marinara sauce
- Olive oil for frying

Instructions:

1. Preheat the oil in a deep fryer or large pot to 350°F (175°C).
2. Roll the pizza dough into small circles, about 4-5 inches in diameter.
3. In a bowl, combine mozzarella, ricotta, and Parmesan cheese.
4. Place a tablespoon of the cheese mixture in the center of each dough circle. Add a teaspoon of marinara sauce on top.
5. Fold the dough over the filling to create a half-moon shape and seal the edges.
6. Fry the panzarotti in the hot oil until golden and crispy, about 3-4 minutes per side.
7. Drain on paper towels and serve hot.

Halloumi Salad (Cyprus)

Ingredients:

- 1 block halloumi cheese, sliced
- 4 cups mixed salad greens
- 1 cup cherry tomatoes, halved
- 1/2 cucumber, sliced
- 1/4 red onion, thinly sliced
- 2 tbsp olive oil
- 1 tbsp lemon juice
- Salt and pepper to taste

Instructions:

1. Heat olive oil in a skillet over medium-high heat. Grill the halloumi slices for 2-3 minutes per side, or until golden and crispy.
2. In a large bowl, combine the salad greens, cherry tomatoes, cucumber, and red onion.
3. Drizzle with olive oil and lemon juice, and season with salt and pepper.
4. Top the salad with the grilled halloumi and serve immediately.

Croquetas de Queso (Spain)

Ingredients:

- 1 cup béchamel sauce (butter, flour, milk)
- 1 1/2 cups manchego cheese, grated
- 1/2 cup breadcrumbs
- 2 eggs, beaten
- Vegetable oil for frying
- Salt and pepper to taste

Instructions:

1. In a saucepan, make the béchamel sauce by melting butter, adding flour, and gradually stirring in the milk until thickened. Season with salt and pepper.
2. Stir in the grated manchego cheese until melted and well combined. Allow the mixture to cool.
3. Once cooled, form the mixture into small balls or cylinders.
4. Dip each croquette into the beaten eggs and coat with breadcrumbs.
5. Heat vegetable oil in a frying pan and fry the croquettes until golden and crispy, about 3-4 minutes.
6. Drain on paper towels and serve warm.

Pizza Quattro Formaggi (Italy)

Ingredients:

- 1 pizza dough (store-bought or homemade)
- 1/2 cup mozzarella cheese, shredded
- 1/2 cup gorgonzola cheese, crumbled
- 1/2 cup ricotta cheese
- 1/2 cup Parmesan cheese, grated
- Olive oil for drizzling
- Fresh basil for garnish

Instructions:

1. Preheat the oven to 475°F (245°C).
2. Roll out the pizza dough on a floured surface and transfer it to a pizza stone or baking sheet.
3. Spread a thin layer of olive oil on the dough and top with the mozzarella, gorgonzola, ricotta, and Parmesan cheeses.
4. Bake the pizza for 10-12 minutes or until the crust is golden and the cheese is bubbling.
5. Remove from the oven and garnish with fresh basil.
6. Slice and serve immediately.

Gratin of Cheese and Potatoes (Switzerland)

Ingredients:

- 4 large potatoes, peeled and sliced
- 1 1/2 cups Gruyère cheese, grated
- 1 cup Emmental cheese, grated
- 1 cup heavy cream
- 1/2 cup milk
- 2 cloves garlic, minced
- Salt and pepper to taste
- Fresh thyme or rosemary for garnish

Instructions:

1. Preheat the oven to 375°F (190°C). Grease a baking dish with butter.
2. Layer the sliced potatoes in the dish, sprinkling each layer with salt, pepper, and garlic.
3. In a separate bowl, mix together the heavy cream and milk. Pour this mixture over the potatoes.
4. Sprinkle the grated Gruyère and Emmental cheese on top of the potatoes.
5. Bake for 45-50 minutes, or until the potatoes are tender and the cheese is golden and bubbling.
6. Garnish with fresh thyme or rosemary and serve hot.

Aged Manchego with Membrillo (Spain)

Ingredients:

- 8 oz aged Manchego cheese, sliced
- 4 oz membrillo (quince paste), sliced
- Fresh walnuts (optional) for garnish

Instructions:

1. Arrange the slices of aged Manchego cheese on a serving platter.
2. Place a slice of membrillo on top or beside each slice of cheese.
3. Optionally, garnish with walnuts for added texture and flavor.
4. Serve as an appetizer or part of a cheese platter.

Tzatziki with Feta (Greece)

Ingredients:

- 1 cup Greek yogurt
- 1/2 cup feta cheese, crumbled
- 1/2 cucumber, finely grated
- 2 cloves garlic, minced
- 1 tbsp lemon juice
- 2 tbsp olive oil
- 1 tbsp fresh dill, chopped
- Salt and pepper to taste

Instructions:

1. In a bowl, combine Greek yogurt, crumbled feta, grated cucumber, garlic, lemon juice, and olive oil.
2. Stir until well combined and season with salt and pepper.
3. Garnish with fresh dill and serve chilled as a dip or sauce.

Cheese Empanadas (Chile)

Ingredients:

- 2 cups all-purpose flour
- 1/2 cup butter, chilled and cut into cubes
- 1/4 cup cold water
- 1 tsp salt
- 1 1/2 cups mozzarella cheese, shredded
- 1/2 cup Parmesan cheese, grated
- 1 egg, beaten (for brushing)

Instructions:

1. In a bowl, combine the flour, salt, and butter. Mix with your fingers until the mixture resembles coarse crumbs.
2. Gradually add cold water, kneading until a dough forms. Wrap and refrigerate for 30 minutes.
3. Preheat the oven to 375°F (190°C).
4. Roll out the dough on a floured surface and cut into circles.
5. Place a small amount of shredded mozzarella and grated Parmesan in the center of each dough circle.
6. Fold the dough over to form a half-moon shape and seal the edges.
7. Brush the empanadas with beaten egg and bake for 15-20 minutes until golden brown.
8. Serve warm as a snack or appetizer.

Blue Cheese Dressing (USA)

Ingredients:

- 1/2 cup mayonnaise
- 1/2 cup sour cream
- 1/4 cup buttermilk
- 1/2 cup blue cheese, crumbled
- 1 tbsp lemon juice
- 1 tsp garlic powder
- Salt and pepper to taste

Instructions:

1. In a bowl, whisk together the mayonnaise, sour cream, buttermilk, and lemon juice.
2. Stir in the crumbled blue cheese and garlic powder.
3. Season with salt and pepper to taste.
4. Chill in the refrigerator for at least 30 minutes before serving as a dressing for salads or as a dipping sauce.

Raclette with Charcuterie (Switzerland)

Ingredients:

- 1 lb Raclette cheese, sliced
- 1 lb assorted charcuterie (prosciutto, salami, etc.)
- 1 baguette, sliced
- 2 cups small potatoes, boiled and halved
- Pickled vegetables (optional)

Instructions:

1. Preheat a raclette grill or a broiler.
2. Arrange the sliced Raclette cheese on the grill trays.
3. Grill the cheese until melted and bubbling, about 5 minutes.
4. Serve the melted cheese over boiled potatoes, charcuterie, and slices of baguette.
5. Optionally, add pickled vegetables on the side for extra flavor.

Saganaki (Greece)

Ingredients:

- 8 oz Kasseri cheese (or any firm, melty cheese)
- 1/4 cup all-purpose flour
- 1 tbsp olive oil
- 1 tbsp lemon juice
- Fresh parsley for garnish

Instructions:

1. Heat olive oil in a pan over medium-high heat.
2. Dredge the cheese slices in flour, shaking off any excess.
3. Fry the cheese in the pan until golden and crispy, about 2-3 minutes per side.
4. Drizzle with lemon juice and garnish with fresh parsley.
5. Serve immediately, often accompanied by bread.

Gougères (France)

Ingredients:

- 1 cup water
- 1/2 cup unsalted butter
- 1 cup all-purpose flour
- 4 large eggs
- 1 1/2 cups Gruyère cheese, grated
- Salt and pepper to taste

Instructions:

1. Preheat the oven to 400°F (200°C). Line a baking sheet with parchment paper.
2. In a saucepan, bring water and butter to a boil. Stir in the flour and cook for 1-2 minutes until the dough pulls away from the sides.
3. Remove from heat and stir in the eggs one at a time until smooth.
4. Fold in the grated Gruyère cheese and season with salt and pepper.
5. Drop spoonfuls of dough onto the prepared baking sheet.
6. Bake for 20-25 minutes, or until golden and puffed up.
7. Serve warm as an appetizer or snack.

Moussaka with Cheese Bechamel (Greece)

Ingredients:

- 2 eggplants, sliced and roasted
- 1 lb ground beef or lamb
- 1 onion, chopped
- 2 cloves garlic, minced
- 1 can (14 oz) crushed tomatoes
- 1 tsp cinnamon
- 1/4 tsp nutmeg
- 2 tbsp olive oil
- 1 cup milk
- 1/4 cup flour
- 1/2 cup grated Parmesan cheese
- 1/2 cup Gruyère cheese, grated
- 2 large eggs, beaten
- Salt and pepper to taste

Instructions:

1. Preheat the oven to 375°F (190°C). Roast the sliced eggplants in olive oil until tender.
2. In a pan, cook the ground meat with onion and garlic until browned. Add crushed tomatoes, cinnamon, nutmeg, salt, and pepper. Simmer for 15-20 minutes.
3. In a saucepan, make the béchamel sauce: melt butter, stir in flour, and gradually add milk. Cook until thickened.
4. Stir in the Parmesan and Gruyère cheeses, followed by the beaten eggs. Season with salt and pepper.
5. In a baking dish, layer the roasted eggplants, followed by the meat sauce, then top with the béchamel sauce.
6. Bake for 30 minutes, or until golden and bubbly. Serve warm.

Cheese-stuffed Peppers (Turkey)

Ingredients:

- 4 large bell peppers (any color)
- 1 cup feta cheese, crumbled
- 1/2 cup rice (cooked)
- 1/2 cup mozzarella cheese, grated
- 1/4 cup parsley, chopped
- 1/2 tsp cumin
- 1/2 tsp paprika
- Salt and pepper to taste
- 1 tbsp olive oil
- 1/4 cup tomato sauce

Instructions:

1. Preheat the oven to 375°F (190°C). Cut the tops off the peppers and remove the seeds.
2. In a bowl, mix the feta cheese, cooked rice, mozzarella, parsley, cumin, paprika, salt, and pepper.
3. Stuff the peppers with the cheese mixture and place them in a baking dish.
4. Drizzle olive oil over the peppers and spoon a little tomato sauce on top.
5. Cover the baking dish with foil and bake for 25-30 minutes, or until the peppers are tender.
6. Serve warm, garnished with extra parsley if desired.

Brie and Fig Tart (France)

Ingredients:

- 1 sheet puff pastry
- 1/2 cup Brie cheese, sliced
- 1/4 cup fig jam
- 1 tbsp honey
- Fresh thyme (optional)
- Salt and pepper to taste

Instructions:

1. Preheat the oven to 400°F (200°C). Roll out the puff pastry on a parchment-lined baking sheet.
2. Spread a thin layer of fig jam over the puff pastry.
3. Arrange the Brie slices on top of the jam.
4. Drizzle honey over the cheese and sprinkle with fresh thyme, salt, and pepper.
5. Bake for 15-20 minutes, or until the pastry is golden and the cheese is melted.
6. Slice and serve warm as an appetizer or light meal.

Panzerotti (Italy)

Ingredients:

- 2 cups all-purpose flour
- 1 tsp salt
- 1 tbsp olive oil
- 1/2 cup warm water
- 1/4 tsp active dry yeast
- 1/2 cup ricotta cheese
- 1/2 cup mozzarella cheese, shredded
- 1/4 cup Parmesan cheese, grated
- 1/4 cup marinara sauce
- Vegetable oil for frying

Instructions:

1. In a bowl, mix flour, salt, and yeast. Add olive oil and warm water, then knead until smooth. Let the dough rise for 1 hour.
2. Roll out the dough into circles and spoon a mixture of ricotta, mozzarella, Parmesan, and a dollop of marinara sauce in the center of each.
3. Fold the dough over the filling to form a half-moon shape and seal the edges tightly.
4. Heat vegetable oil in a deep pan and fry the panzerotti until golden brown, about 4-5 minutes per side.
5. Drain on paper towels and serve with extra marinara sauce for dipping.

Shepherd's Pie with Cheese (UK)

Ingredients:

- 1 lb ground lamb (or beef for cottage pie)
- 1 onion, chopped
- 2 carrots, diced
- 1/2 cup peas
- 2 cloves garlic, minced
- 1 tbsp tomato paste
- 1 cup beef broth
- 2 tbsp Worcestershire sauce
- 4 cups mashed potatoes
- 1/2 cup cheddar cheese, grated
- Salt and pepper to taste

Instructions:

1. Preheat the oven to 400°F (200°C).
2. In a large skillet, brown the ground meat with onions, carrots, and garlic. Add tomato paste, Worcestershire sauce, and beef broth. Simmer for 10 minutes until thickened.
3. Stir in peas and season with salt and pepper.
4. Transfer the meat mixture into a baking dish and top with mashed potatoes. Sprinkle grated cheddar cheese on top.
5. Bake for 20 minutes, or until the top is golden and bubbly.
6. Serve warm as a comforting main dish.

Queso a la Plancha (Mexico)

Ingredients:

- 8 oz firm white cheese (like queso panela or halloumi)
- 1 tbsp olive oil
- 1/4 tsp chili powder
- Fresh cilantro for garnish
- Lime wedges

Instructions:

1. Slice the cheese into thick pieces.
2. Heat olive oil in a skillet over medium heat.
3. Place the cheese slices in the skillet and cook for 2-3 minutes per side, or until golden brown and crispy.
4. Sprinkle with chili powder and garnish with fresh cilantro.
5. Serve with lime wedges for squeezing over the cheese.

Pasticciotto (Italy)

Ingredients:

- 2 cups all-purpose flour
- 1/2 cup sugar
- 1/2 cup unsalted butter, softened
- 2 large eggs
- 1/2 tsp vanilla extract
- 1/4 tsp baking powder
- 1/4 cup milk
- 1 cup ricotta cheese
- 1/2 cup powdered sugar
- 1/2 tsp lemon zest

Instructions:

1. Preheat the oven to 350°F (175°C). Grease a muffin tin or individual tart pans.
2. In a bowl, mix flour, sugar, and baking powder. Add butter, eggs, and vanilla and mix until smooth.
3. Divide the dough into individual portions and press into the muffin tin or tart pans.
4. In a separate bowl, mix ricotta cheese, powdered sugar, and lemon zest.
5. Spoon the ricotta mixture into the dough-filled molds.
6. Bake for 20-25 minutes, or until golden brown.
7. Let cool before serving.

www.ingramcontent.com/pod-product-compliance
Lightning Source LLC
LaVergne TN
LVHW081500060526
838201LV00056BA/2852